Home to
Each Other
and more moments
of everyday grace

Margaret Cessna, H.M.

Home to Each Other

Cover Art: Paulette Kirschensteiner

To order additional copies, please contact us.
www.CreateSpace.com

For my brothers
Jim, Jack and Tom

And in loving memory of our brothers
Bob and Bill

Sam Fulwood III wrote:
All writers tell stories. Good writers draw stories from life.
Outstanding writers spin the hardships of their own woes into
revelations that help all of us see the world more clearly.

Hopefully, I have been able to fulfill some of
these guidelines.

Prologue

Many of the chapters in this book have appeared first in other publications. I decided to pull them all together and then add a few more.

I believe that seemingly little moments often lead to valuable insights. A young girl's desire to help poor children. An old woman's devotion to authenticity. A grandma's love. I am sharing some of these insights here.

I also believe that some of the darkest moments offer enormous grace. Death and dying. Struggling with faith. Overcoming fear. These moments are here, too.

And, finally, I believe that through some specific personal experiences we are able to understand that we are not alone in these moments and that there are profound lessons available for all of us and for each of us. Human experience after all is human experience and most of what we sample in life does not belong to anyone alone. Life belongs to all of us. I find comfort in knowing that others understand my joy and my grief because of their own joy and their own grief.

Margaret Cessna, HM
Lakewood, Ohio

Table of Contents

Children

Faith

Musings

Strangers in a Strange Land

Home

Thank You

Children

The Hearts of Children

A week after my grand niece Morgan's seventh birthday in October, she told me that she had $50.00 and was saving her money. She wanted to buy a water slide for her back yard. She needed $350.00 more and knew that it would take a long time to reach her goal, but at seven she had already learned the discipline of saving for something that she really wanted. Last year she saved every quarter and dollar that she got for her birthday and from the Tooth Fairy, from her grandparents, mom, dad, aunts and uncles so that she could buy and Build A Bear. She got her bear. A water slide would take a little longer but Morgan was confident that she could do it.

In the meantime, my family is very supportive of Heifer International and their program of providing animals to families that are poor all over the world. We have exchanged Heifer animals at Christmas time for years. We did so again this year but added a new element. It was decided to do a joint project that would include both adults and kids. We would have the opportunity to donate all through the year to raise money for Heifer. A money jar was fixed for the donations and the photo of a little girl from Peru with her arm around a llama was taped on the jar. Together we would buy a llama.

A chart went up on the refrigerator with one hundred and fifty blocks. Every time a dollar was donated, one block would be colored. Minimum donation was 25¢ for one fourth of a block. Once we reached $150.00 we would buy a llama. Not as a gift. We would buy a llama just because we wanted to. Just because we liked the picture of the little girl now taped to our money jar. When that was done, we would start over with another chart and another photo on the money jar.

We gathered on Christmas day for our family celebration, exchanged our Heifer cards, and then watched the kids open family presents. Our traditional Christmas meal was laced with discussion about our new project. The jar and the chart were successfully begun with some initial donations.

By Christmas, Morgan's fortune had grown to $70.00.

The day after Christmas Morgan's mom told me that Morgan wanted to put all of her $70.00 into the jar to buy a llama for that little girl on the money jar. She was dollar savvy and knew that she would be a full year behind in her quest for a water slide. She was willing and eager to do just that.

Her mother wisely told her that if she did that then the rest of us would not have as much of a chance to help. She understood. Seven years old and she understood. Seven years and two months.

She put her dollar into the jar and colored in one of the blocks. She was satisfied with leaving something for others in the family to contribute. Smiling she said that was only the first time. She would put a little more in later.

So thank you, Morgan, and all of you children who collected money and socks and toys for the victims of Katrina and the tsunami before that. Thanks to all of you young boys who shaved your heads when a pal was going through chemo. Thanks as well to all of the young women who had bake sale after bake sale to help find a cure for breast cancer. We pin our hopes on you. You show us the way and light our path. You bless us and maybe, even, you will save us.

It has been claimed that if women were in charge of the world there would be peace on earth and war no more. I think that, perhaps, if we follow the hearts of the children, no one would ever be hungry or poor again.

Lost in a World of Plenty

I was more than surprised when I saw that the final exam was on fire. I rushed to Joe's desk to smother the fire with a book.

"Why'd you do that, Joe?" I asked.

"Didn't know any answers," he said.

His behavior effectively ended final exam class as every eye in the room was on Joe and me. The desk in front of him was vacant so I sat down sideways and turned to face him.

"Well, what do we do now?" I whispered.

"I don't care," he sighed. "I don't care."

Joe didn't need punishment. Although his face was the picture of innocence, his life had been a battlefield. For years he had been in a combat ready stance with no relief for refreshing rest. He had been defeated by grief and despair. Only God knows for how long. He didn't care much about passing his final exam, but he cared enough to try to destroy the evidence of his failure. He was only fifteen years old.

I collected all of the unfinished exams and finished the class with discussion and said I would give each student a grade for participation and insight. The kids were jumping out of their seats to participate, evidently grateful that there was no written exam. Grateful that their classroom had not been incinerated. Even more grateful that their pal, Joe, was just sitting quietly. After class Joe and I walked together to the school office.

The next week I visited him in the psych ward at the hospital. We didn't talk. Just walked up and down the halls. He didn't say he was glad that I was there but he never asked me to leave him alone. I told him that I would be moving to another town in a week. I promised that I would be thinking of him and wishing him well. I have kept that promise for a long time.

He was a lost soul. Well, who isn't? What separates me, and I suspect many of us, from Joe is simply degree. How does anyone truly find his or her way? How do I find my way in a world where countries are invaded for no clear reason? Where a father sends a pit bull after his son to teach him a lesson? Where the environment is evaporating around us and at the same time unseasonable rains flood every valley? Where I hold the hand of my mother whom I have loved without measure and watch her die slowly and painfully? Where we have money for war as the elderly struggle to pay for medications? Where the Church makes no sense and covers up its sins? Where the spirits of the young are beaten down by bureaucrats who pretend that they care? How do I find my way in a world where bombs get more attention than schools?

It surprises me that with all that I do not believe, I am not yet ready to give up on angels. And I need some angels here. Some guardian angels to keep me on the straight and narrow. To help me stay focused on the truth that I have been saved. If only from myself. If only from the fear of failure. To keep me from setting my dreams on fire. To help me protect my energy so that I stay on the path. So that I don't lose my way. So that I am not lost.

I have never been able to find out what became of Joe. I hope an angel found him and that he was able to recover his self. The one that was created for happiness and freedom. Freedom from being a lost boy in a world that never seemed to care.

Throw Away Kids

They were my boys. All twenty-two of them. I'm not sure why we clicked but it may have been because I did not think of them or treat them like crops that needed to be rotated. That's what their science teacher told them when he changed his seating plan. Classes were grouped according to ability. They were on the bottom of the bottom. And they knew it.

I found out that for most of them it was not a matter of ability but rather a lack of motivation. They could focus when they wanted. They could remember when they were interested.

They were tough street kids and almost all of them smoked. It was a while ago and a funny school rule allowed boys to smoke in the parking lot at lunch time. Being a former smoker, I knew what that break meant to them. So I built on a carrot that I dangled in front of them every day. If they were appropriate in their behavior and at least feigned interest in the lesson, I would dismiss them two minutes before the bell. Lunch followed class and this way they could be first in line in the cafeteria, gulp their lunch and make it to the parking lot in time for an few extra puffs. If they were inappropriate or uninterested, I held them two minutes after the end of class. They then had to choose between food and nicotine.

I held them late very few times. As they left early, part of the deal was that they had to escape undetected by anyone in the adjacent classrooms. It was a sight to see - these hulking almost-men tiptoeing silently to the stairs and down. They knew that if anyone found out about our pact they would be doomed. Along with me.

Magic happened in that room.

"Take a break, Sis," Tom would say. "I'll set up the projector and run the film for you." He became the "projo man."

Frank whispered one day before class, "Ron's brother was in a car wreck last night so he might not be able to pay attention today. Go easy with him."

I don't think he knew that I was a racing fan the day Dominic asked at the beginning of class, "So who do you like in the Derby?"

I gave him an assignment and the next day he put a chart on the side board listing the jockeys, entries, post position and odds. He spent a few minutes explaining odds and told his students they had twenty-four hours to make their picks. Anyone who had the winner would get a weekend without homework.

"And by the way," he said, "read the paper before you pick your horse."

Dennis showed me an ad from an auto magazine.

"This is the car I'm going to buy as soon as I get a job."

I suggested that would be a great reward to give himself when he finished college. But we both knew he would never cross the threshold of advanced education. My earnest hope was that he would cross the high school stage to pick up his diploma. The odds were not in his favor.

Jerry sat in the last seat of the row. His gym towel was on the floor under his desk. His buddy across the aisle grabbed the towel, flipped it against the floor and the contents rolled to the front of the room. I told Jerry, who was in obvious pain, not to worry. I had five brothers and had seen athletic supporters before.

These were throw away kids. They were not scholars or athletes. Not debaters or thespians. No student council or class office positions for them. More often than not, they were in detention after school or the principal's office during the day. My sense was that they had experienced a lot in their young lives. Except for kindness. They were not used to someone being kind to them. What I found out about them is that they all had hearts the size of Wyoming. Their response to my kindness was kindness. They went out of their way to help me. They relaxed in my presence as I did in theirs. We had a good time.

I was fair with them and offered to help them in any way that I could. They knew what I expected. They were hoping for D's. I was hoping for C's and B's because I knew that they could do it. They all passed. None with flying colors. But pass they did.

I do not pretend to think that eighteen weeks in my classroom was a transforming experience for them. It was, however, a transforming experience for me. They taught me as much as I taught them. I learned in a brand new way that kindness works. Fairness works. I learned that there is no such thing as a throw away kid. That sometimes it takes as little as a bet on the Derby to break through tough exteriors. They allowed me a glance at hearts that hungered for something as simple as a little deal that worked in their favor. They were not used to that. They gobbled it up. Showed up for class. At least looked interested. Got their smokes. Engraved themselves indelibly on my memory. They were my boys. And, honest to God, they made me love them.

His Name Is Juan

He is twelve years old and in the sixth grade. With soft curly hair, the face of an angel and a million dollar smile, I could imagine him being dubbed "Mr. Hollywood" somewhere down the road. Probably will not happen. My hope for him is that he isn't lost in a school system that caters to standardized test scores and keeping violence at a minimum.

His name is Juan but his brother told me to call him John. He prefers Juan. So Juan it is. When he signed up for my Creative Writing class at an after school teen center, I asked him why he was interested when he could have been in the gym playing basketball.

"I like to write," he said, "what are we going to write about?"

In the middle of a decaying, urban neighborhood, "I like to write," is what I heard and my heart jumped in my chest as I considered all of the possibilities for this beautiful young man. No armor encased him. He was wide open, ready to dive into anything new that would broaden his world and give him some sense of accomplishment. He couldn't articulate that but everything about him told me that it was so.

I then addressed the class and told them about an accomplished American writer.

"Susan Sontag is her name," I told them. "She was being interviewed and was asked why she wrote. One of the main reasons was because there were things that she wanted the world to know."

"You have something to say to the world as well," I said. "What is it that you want the world to know? About you, your family, your school, your neighborhood? What do you want the world to know about your dreams? What is it that we must tell the world so that they know? So that they care? Think about that for a few weeks."

Back to Juan. He told me that he lived nine blocks from the center and I suggested that it took him a long time to make the trip every day.

"No, no," he said, "I know all of the shortcuts. Besides, I like coming here."

He nibbled on the CHEEZ-ITs and ate the yogurt that I brought to class as he filled out the introductory form. He couldn't spell the name of his middle school. After I told him to sound it out, he came close to being correct. He completed the sentence stems that I had given to him and we went over them together.

Being a "cope" was his life goal. When I asked him why, he told me that sometimes policemen give people a second chance and to him that was very important. Helping his mother made him happy. I asked him to explain. What surprised me is that he didn't say that he had eight sisters and brothers. He said that his mother had nine kids.

"My mother has nine kids so sometimes I cook. That makes her happy."

His favorite is red beans, rice and pork. I now have the recipe.

Sadness surrounds me as I think about his face, about his dream, about his recipe for red beans, rice and pork. Hope for him is trying to break through for me but the reality is that he will most probably be another failing test score that is passed from grade to grade so that when he finishes high school he still will not be able to spell the name of his middle school. We will work to make sure that doesn't happen. To make sure that he will be able to spell the name of his school.

In the meantime, I have him for a full hour every week. We will work on spelling and on writing. He will eat the snacks as he continues to think about his long-term assignment, as he thinks about what he wants the world to know. I am confident that there will be wisdom in his words. Perhaps a little courage, too. Then we will work to try to figure out together how we will get the world to listen.

Emily

On Friday a friend told me that she hadn't taken time to grieve.

"I've been too busy," she said, "and I know that I need to make time."

I spent the next forty-eight hours, waking and sleeping, trying to figure out what that meant. Taking the time to grieve. Grief is no stranger to me. It is real. Sickness. Death. Loss. All at once, it seems. I finish a good book and want to call my mother to see if she wants to read it. We have always shared good books. But her dementia is so advanced that she sometimes doesn't even know who I am. I hear a certain strain of music and I think of my musician brother, dead last year at too early an age. A good friend died last year and I still have her phone number on my speed dial.

My grief is close. Always with me. Have I taken the time to grieve? How does one do that? Especially when it is always present. Knowing that it will not always be as intense. But always present. Coloring all days and nights. I have to give myself time to grieve. But what other time is there besides every minute of the day and night?

She was dressed in a pink velour jacket. Light brown hair fell below her collar. She was in the pew ahead of me. This beautiful child became my focus during Mass and she herself was my prayer as I joined her in marveling at color transforming paper. She was coloring a cowboy. A cowboy playing a guitar. It filled her moment and mine as well. The moment was all we had as one blended into another interrupted only by music from the choir.

Yahweh, I know you are near, standing always
by my side.
You guard me from the foe, and you lead me in
ways everlasting.

Her innocence was so pure that it was piercing. My grief was momentarily suspended somewhere beyond her face.

She sat on the kneeler, the pew her desk. Her crayons were lined up in an orderly, executive manner. I was fascinated by her color selection. The choices of blue, purple and pink were very striking.

Out of the corner of my ear I heard "faith, hope and love, and the greatest of these is love."

And I thought of the joy, peace, innocence that I was experiencing in her as I watched.

Joy, peace, innocence - and grief. And the deepest of these is grief. Joy, peace and innocence will come and go. Grief you will always have with you. But this child does not yet know this.

Blessed are they, full of sorrow, they shall be consoled.
Rejoice and be glad! Blessed are you, holy are you!
Rejoice and be glad, yours is the kingdom of God.

She stood on her desk chair and faced the altar when the bells rang to announce the bread of life and the cup of salvation. No more bells so she sat again and finished coloring the man with the guitar. She carefully tore the sheet from her coloring book and put it in the pew by her dad.

Awake from your slumber!
Arise from your sleep.
A new day is dawning for all those who weep.
Let us build the city of God,
May our tears be turned into dancing!

After Mass, I introduced myself to her dad.

"Her name is Emily," he said, "and she is four years old."

I asked Emily if I could have her picture to hang on my refrigerator. When she looked at her dad with a big question on her face, he said,

"I know you did it for me but you can give it to Peg."

"No, no, no," I said. "That would not be ok."

I told Emily that I was glad she had done the picture for her dad and that I enjoyed seeing it. I turned to put my coat on and when I looked back, Emily was handing me a new picture that she had quickly done with just a few strokes of red. Overwhelmed by the generosity of this little person, I thanked her and told her that red was my favorite color and that I would put it on my refrigerator. Which I did. And it serves to remind me that there is more to life than grief. There is joy, peace, innocence as well.

I came to realize in those moments on a Sunday morning that the question is not about taking time to grieve. The question, for me, is how to take time out of grieving to appreciate the beauty, peace and rhythm of life. In this case, found in the form of a kindhearted little girl. Emily is her name and she turned my tears into dancing.

Faith

The Way of Luella

As I find myself struggling more and more with what seem to be primitive dogma, rules and regulations of a Church that belongs to other centuries, Luella walked into my life. The depth of her wholeness, of her holiness near took my breath away. At eighty-three, she is a self-proclaimed survivor who has emerged from the grief and suffering of most of her life with grace and gentility. She is a walking Gospel giving life to the teachings of Jesus in the most simple and meaningful ways.

"It was bad," she would say in describing the difficulties of growing up black in the Deep South. "But, look at me. I am still standing and I am filled with gratitude."

She wanted to write her story so that her grand-children and great grandchildren would know where they came from. She wanted them to know that endurance is a good thing. That pain is a part of life. That pain can touch their hearts and their souls. That pain, however, does not ever need to defeat them or define them.

Luella is short of stature and ramrod straight. Her mind is sharp and her memory clear. And of no small consequence, she is a great hugger.

I met her every week to take notes as she told me her story. I would organize it for her, scan her photos, and turn her conversations with me into a narrative that she could pass on to her loved ones. When we finished, I handed her six simply bound copies of her work. She thanked me over and over. I had to remind her over and over that telling her story was a gift to me and that our every moment together was precious grace.

Getting to know Luella and to experience her deep faith and positive outlook reminded me that living the Gospel is more important than trying to figure out why some teachings just do not seem to fit anymore. Luella bears no hostility. So why should I allow myself frustration and anger.

"Do what she does," I say to myself.

Be grateful. Be kind. Be loving. Be generous. Leave the dogma to others. It is easy to be frustrated with dogma and practice. Being grateful and kind, loving and generous is not always easy. But that's the way of Luella. And she is still standing.

So during this time of turbulence in the world and chaos in the Church, I have decided to take my guidance from Luella.

"Walk with dignity and grace," she would tell me, "and know that frustration and pain do not need to defeat you or define who you are."

Luella has led me to a birth of new energy so I think that sort of makes me her child now, too. Following her example, I will rely on the message of the Gospels to lead me. I will embrace endurance and pay no attention to the nasty demon of anger.

For everything there is a season. And a time for every purpose under heaven. But, oh, how I wish that I had met her earlier.

Meatballs or Crab Cakes

It was a Friday during Lent. Four of us had met for lunch together as we often did. This was an Italian restaurant new to us and I was forever in search of the perfect meatball. I wanted to order pasta with meatballs. The crab cakes would have tasted just as good. No sacrifice there. It was 2008, after all, and had we not emerged from an immature position in our Church to become adults in charge of our own souls? Our own menus? Besides, the crab cakes honestly would have tasted just as good, I told them.

Her response stayed with me much longer than the taste of a new Italian restaurant.

"What makes us holy?" she asked, as I sampled a meatball and she her crab cake.

A good question for all four of us since we each had been in pursuit of holiness, of wholeness, for almost a half a century each.

Fork in mid air, I looked at her and then at the others. I ate the bite, put my fork down and we talked. As we had done for years. Four friends looking for goodness. Relying on each other for guidance, support, insight, and feedback. Meatballs on a Friday during Lent or Maryland crab cakes. Doesn't really matter. We had never been in the habit of judging each other. We were not about to start now.

What is it that makes us holy? It is about doing the best we can, we decided. To be kind and courageous. To help those we can. To be unselfish. To get up when we fall down. To start over when we fail. To believe that it is possible to love one another even when we have a hard time doing it.

I will not judge you as you eat your meatball and I my crab cake. There are issues that demand more attention than a taste of meat on a Friday in Lent. And we were launched once again into problem solving for the world's hungry children, for women who are abused every day and for the people who call a steam grate on a downtown street "home" for the night. We were frustrated about the disease carried around the world by impure water that would be so easy to make clean. Would eradicating poverty be more effective in defeating terrorism than bombs? Of course it would. Any thinking person knows that. And on and on and on.

No dessert today. Just hugs all around and urgings to "take care of yourself. See you next time."

The ride home was a long one and during that time I mused about my need to convince my pals, and perhaps myself as well, that crab cakes would have tasted just as good. The old Catholic stomach had kicked in again, as I had a split second recall about what we had been taught would happen to you if you ate meat on Friday. Any Friday.

I reminded myself that God surely has better things to pay attention to. I told myself that God has absolutely nothing to do with this choice. Nothing. God does not care. When I am in my right mind I would never spend time or energy thinking about things like this.

As I pulled into my driveway, I finally admitted to myself that the crab cakes would have been a better choice. If I had ordered them, my mind would have been free. Free to think of lots of other things on the way home. Free to think of things that were kind, courageous, helpful, unselfish, loving, enduring. Things that solved problems for the hungry, the abused, the homeless, the sick, the poor. Things that could make a difference. On a Friday in Lent. In the year of Our Lord, 2008.

The Passions of the Christ

I went to Mass last Sunday and saw the Gospel. A young mother with three children sat two pews in front of me. The pew between was empty so I could enjoy them without interference. The youngest was a boy in a baby carrier about the size of a manger. The lining was blue and quilted, soft and thick. No straw in sight. His sister attended to this boy child with reverence, awe and tenderness. She was a few years younger than Mary of Nazareth would have been on the day that she gave birth. Occasionally, the older son reached down so that his little brother could grab his finger. The mother was in a state of constant awareness and affection.

I was pleasantly distracted by this baby. And as I watched him and his mom, sister and brother, I wondered how this child would be saved from being selfish and if he might some day deliver us, too. Possibly from cancer, from terrorism, from ignorance. Would he be a doctor, a lawyer, a teacher, an elected official? A loving son, then an honorable man?

The child was the homily for me last Sunday. Would he ever understand that we are called to save ourselves from sin because we have a model to show the way? Would he understand that we are called to save each other from sin with the help of the life and teachings of a humble man centuries removed yet present to us always?

Would this child ever be nailed to the cross of discrimination, racism, homophobia? Would mean classmates form his sense of self? Would pop culture prompt him to embrace violence as a way of life? Or would a loving village show him the way to happiness that comes from a life well lived, characterized by love, generosity and service. Would he learn to be courageous in times of trouble and hold his ground in the face of malice?

His potential for goodness is boundless. I dismissed the negative and focused on what was before me. Two pews ahead. The circle of life personified. A new being, waiting to be formed by the love that was surrounding him.

For a moment my gaze shifted to the very large crucifix that was hanging in the front of the church. And I asked myself, what in the Gospel commands us to worship the flayed skin and broken body of Jesus, the Christ? Should we stop focusing on the less than twenty-four hours that Jesus was tortured and crucified during his physical suffering? It doesn't seem right. Shouldn't we pay more attention to the other passions that he spent three years sharing with all of us who care to notice?

Should we focus instead on his passion for children - that they be treated well? On his empathy with his friends when their brother died? Should we look at how he fed the hungry and urged us to do likewise? Should we not look at how he erased the line of hatred between Jews and Samaritans when he asked, simply, for a drink of water as he sat by the well at mid-day? What about his generosity and his kindness? The way he honored his parents? How he loved his friends?

My hope, my prayer for this young boy, two pews ahead, is that he is blessed with hearts around him that love him to completion. That form him in kindness and generosity. That show him the way to be a whole person in love with life. In love with the heavens and earth that surround him. My hope and my prayer is that he, too, will grow in wisdom and grace. And is that not what the gospels are about?

And so, as this family was the Gospel and the homily, they were also the final blessing. Urging me to go forth and to do in my life what my prayer and hope are for the child. The Mass is ended. Go in peace to love and serve the Lord. Amen. Alleluia.

Mother Cabrini's Head

It was the head that really got to me. It was wax. I had approached the sanctuary after Mass at the Shrine of Mother Cabrini in Manhattan to view her glass-encased body. Her body was there, the sign said, but her head was reconstructed of wax.

"Who decided that?" I wondered. "Why would God preserve her and not other holy people? Surely a personal God, a God who is involved in every life, would not play favorites. And what was that about her head?"

There was no one to ask, so after I got home, I called the shrine to find out about it. I called on a weekday during business hours. This was their business, after all. An elderly-sounding woman answered the phone. I told her about my questions.

"Oh, honey," she said, "it is just one of those crazy things that the church does."

She told me that Mother Cabrini's head and hands were in her hometown in Italy and the rest of her was at the shrine in New York.

"We have most of the bones," she said, "and her hometown has the rest. They wanted to have something and that is what they got."

When I asked if the shrine had only bones or if the body had been preserved, she said, "I think there is a little bit of skin. They open the glass every six years, you know, to make sure that she is OK."

The 15-minute experience in the shrine catapulted me on a long and lonesome journey of wondering about a personal God. And about Mother Cabrini's head.

When I was young, I was taught that this personal God hears every prayer, gives everyone the same chances and rewards, and punishes all according to the same guidelines. My faith was one of comfort and fervor. But as I grew up, I began to question what seemed to be too-simple answers about faith, prayer and God.

What is there to think and believe about a God who would sort of preserve a saint and not preserve everyone, so that all who loved them could continue to revere their sort-of-preserved remains? Maybe I shouldn't be placing this responsibility on any god at all. There is, however, a residue from my earlier days of reading the lives of the saints. And what I had learned is that only God can preserve bodies, and when it happened a saint was proclaimed. As I stood there looking at the remains, I thought about what I don't believe anymore.

I sometimes yearn for that lost simplicity that governs the belief in the guidance of the Holy Spirit, in the unchanging position that my personal prayer can heal all of the sick, feed all of the hungry, end all of the wars.

The roots of my faith are becoming brittle and dry. And yet I can almost feel them stretching down in search of new waters of eternal life. Perhaps the remnants of that faith are what prompt the deep need to find a new source of belief and comfort.

My sometime hope is that I will have a satori moment when I say, "Oh, yes. That's the answer."

But I know it doesn't work that way, I know it is a process. Maybe that's the answer: that there are no easy answers. The struggle adds depth. The seeking adds substance.

I don't think transformation only happens at baptism. I think it happens on a day-to-day, sometimes hour-to-hour or even minute-by-minute basis. Then, before sleep comes, it is possible to pray for fortitude and courage for the next day and in thanksgiving for another day that allowed me the opportunity to be sincere in my wonderings, in my prayer, in my desire to find the home where my heart belongs and where my spirit will thrive. Grateful for another day of trying to do my best. Of sincerely searching for the way that I am called to be good. To be human. To be holy.

Rilke is probably right when he says that we will "live one day into the answer."

So thank you, Mother Cabrini. Even though I don't understand why your body is in New York and your head is in Italy, I am grateful that experiencing the sight of your New York remains caught me off-guard and launched me on a quest for a deeper and more meaningful faith. A new search for a personal God.

In the meantime, look out, Mother Teresa. Be prepared for the global struggle over your bones.

Thoughts from an Airport
While Waiting for a Delayed Flight

My flight was cancelled. Technical problems, they said. So I didn't mind waiting a few hours for a trouble-free plane.

I had been thinking about the announcements that I heard at Mass last week. We were told what to do with our arms and hands. At that moment, I thought of Nero playing his fiddle. While Rome burned. I hadn't had time to think much about it before I left for this trip. Now would be a good time with no interruptions. Pencil in hand, I began to write on the back of my e-ticket pages.

Will transubstantiation go the way of limbo? What about intinction? Truth or myth? Comfort or control? Why do I feel so isolated in feeling and thinking that we have been duped? By the closed and most entrenched system in the world. Maybe even in history. But here is something new: stand up, sit down, extend your hands palms up for prayer. Cosmetic adjustments that do not fool many of us. A shot of spiritual botox where it has no meaning and changes nothing.

This is a faith and a church into which I was born. A church and a faith that nourished me and formed me. So why do I feel so empty when the arguments used are so silly?

Empty pews make me think more and more are catching on. But there are still many in the pews. Including me, sometimes. Is it fear or need for community? I still feel drained. And manipulated.

Some say the brain literally craves a force other than I – a transcendent presence – a need to recognize a power greater than oneself. A way to explain the pull to the heavens, to the stars.

Did we come from the stars as some claim? Are we truly stardust? Will we return to the same source? Will we all meet again?

Do we need a programmed way to understand what it means to be good? Or is it inside of each of us? Do we need a heaven to reach for to keep us on the straight and narrow? Do we need a way to tally good and bad so that we feel safe on the journey to wherever? Do we need a class system to keep us in line in order to preserve our hope for something better beyond this life?

Is it as simple as having a formal way to confess sorrow and regret? But who does that anymore? Bless me friend for I have sinned. Thanks for being so forgiving. Let's have a cup of coffee. And maybe a cookie. Or a piece of fudge. Don't need the confessional anymore. But the sacrament remains.

Till death do us part unless you have the dough and the energy for an annulment. Can't we just admit that sometimes divorce is a healthy choice? That another chance at happiness and fulfillment could be well deserved?

Meatless Fridays in Lent only recommended. Do they know that they are losing their grip? And where will we turn when the grip is truly lost?

Yet in some ways I am still hooked. When the celebration is good there is nothing like it. No fire and brimstone. Music and dance (as long as I don't have to dance). Fellowship. Sisterhood. Peace be with you. Really, I mean it. How can I help? Is there anything that you need? Peace be with you.

If only those at the top would mingle, really mingle with those of us on the bottom there might be some hope. If only those at the top would embrace those of us at the bottom with some warmth, there might be some comfort. If only the playing field could be leveled. If only the praying field could be leveled. If only there were no top and no bottom, perhaps hands and hearts could be joined in a grand circle of love and life and hope. In the meantime, I am left with an emptiness that was once filled with loyalty, pride and a deep sense of belonging. It is an isolating feeling that I have no time to reverse today because my plane is now ready for departure and I need to board for the long trip home.

Stardust

Shakespeare wrote, "When he shall die, take him and cut him out in little stars, and he will make the face of heaven so fine that all the world will be in love with night, and pay no worship to the garish sun"*

In a dream, I sent a questionnaire to God and asked for it to be filled in. Where do people go after they die? Will I see them again? What is this all about, anyway? Tell me everything. Please.

The questionnaire came back blank. If God would not fill it in for me, who will?

People I have loved for so long have died. And I want to know where they are now. I want to know. I want to see them again. To believe that I will see them again lessens the heartache of loss at least a little.

Star light, star bright
First star I see tonight
I wish I may, I wish I might
Have this wish I wish tonight

To know is my wish for tonight. To know is always my wish.

I know what I want the answer to be. I wondered if there was someone, anyone who could provide some clues or answers. I cannot be the only one with this question.

Some say that we are made of stardust. They make that claim based on the fact that every atom in our bodies, other than hydrogen, was fashioned in the fire of stars.

If we are stardust where and on whom will we shine? In the rays of what sun do we sparkle? Does our dust float? Do we know in the grains of our stardust that we are not at all temporary? That we are as eternal as the heavens? Do we never dim, never go the way of a dying nova? Once returned to the heavens do we wait patiently for our own to be returned to us that we may continue to shine together on all those who still have claim to our love? To our faithfulness? To our goodness? Our goodness that is an extension of the very goodness of God?

And, oh, yes, will we each one night be an evening star that earthlings wish upon?

Don't the heavens have enough stars already?

I received a sympathy card from a friend when my mother died with these comforting words of St. John Chrysostom : "They whom we love and lose are no longer where they were before. They are now wherever we are."

How did he know that? By looking at the nighttime sky? Did his questionnaire to God come back filled in?

I wondered about all of this once again when my brother Bobby died recently.

I don't know, but I suspect, that during the last days or perhaps hours, the dying inhabit two worlds. The here and the beyond. And I suspect that once they understand that those left behind will be o.k., they jump at the chance to move to the next step. I suspect that because of the peace that I experienced in Bobby who had told me exactly one year before he died that he was terrified of death and asked me if I was terrified, too. I told him that I was not afraid. I suspect these things but I do not know.

"What if there is nothing beyond this life?" he asked me. "I just cannot deal with the thought of nothing."

I told him that if there was nothing he would never know it. I did tell him, however, that if there was something that he would be in for a marvelous adventure and journey. That our loved ones who went before would be waiting for him. He was not ill at the time so our conversation did not pose any immediacy. We explored all of the possibilities and I think it made a difference to him.

I have these thoughts because he was close to death during our last visit, our last good-bye. He was different then. He was coherent but did not have much energy and was not able to converse much. He listened, though, and let me know that he heard me and understood me. He was not in pain, was peaceful and did not seem to be afraid. He did tell me that he knew the end of this part of his journey was close. It was clear to me then that he was brave enough to die. I was so proud of him and moved by his sense of trust in what was to be. My last words whispered in his ear were that I would see him again.

There was a little smile on his face the moment that he died. I continue to wonder what it was that caused that smile.

And I know that I am not the only one besides Shakespeare who thinks about life after death. Aristotle wrote, "whatsoever that be within us that feels, thinks, desires, and animates, is something celestial, divine, and consequently imperishable."

And Lord Byron: "Immortality o'ersweeps all pains, all tears, all time, all fears, and peals, like the eternal thunder of the deep, into my ears this truth: Thou livest forever!"

"In the wreck of noble lives something immortal still survives." Henry Wadsworth Longfellow. But where and how?

The Church has taught for centuries that we are dust and unto dust we shall return. And that we will rise again in glory.

And then there are those who have recently introduced the idea of stardust. I know there are other traditions as well that consider reincarnation, karma and nothingness.

Whom shall we believe? Who has a line on the real truth? I really want an answer here.

There seem to be many who think that we mortals are not mortal after all. We do live on somehow, somewhere. That is the one part of the mystery that we Christians collectively seem to have. The mystery survives.

In the end, for me, it comes down to belief. Belief that we live on eternally and that we will see once again the faces of those that we have loved. I wish I had more. But I don't. So believe I will. At least for today. Please God, don't let me be wrong.

  * _Romeo and Juliet_

Musings

Faithful Servant

"Let's have a cozy, Darlin'," she would say and then we would have a bit of tea and a bunch of conversation. In her lilting brogue she would remind me that life was lovely and aren't we lucky to have this time together. She was a master at "letting it go" because negative responses would interfere with the lovely memories that we were making.

She came into this world as Margaret O'Brien in County Clare, Ireland. She left this world ninety-three years later as Sister Vincent de Paul O'Brien in Villa Maria, Pennsylvania.

Vincent was my friend and if I were pope, I would "sancto subito." Saint Vincent de Paul II.

She left her beloved Ireland as a young girl to find work as a domestic in New York in order to send money home. Having cousins in Cleveland she joined them for a while and then entered the Sisters of the Humility of Mary in 1929 and faithfully served for seventy years.

Having very little formal education, she did not pursue studies once she made her vows. She became dorm mother at the community boarding school and served in that capacity for thirty years. She loved the young people and was friend, counselor and yes, confessor, to multitudes of students, parents and friends who kept in touch with her years after their school days. No one knows how many and can only guess based on the volume of her visits, phone calls, and mail.

She became Executive Housekeeper at the motherhouse when she left the school. Titles were not important to her. She just mopped and cleaned and dusted and worked with the hired help for twenty-two years.

As a student of the gospels she lived her life simply, prayerfully and generously. Her influence was both gentle and powerful. She exuded gratitude for all of the blessings in her life and taught many of us to do the same. To sip a cup with her and to listen to her would make one think that abundant blessings were the only things worth our attention.

She was calm and soothing, this daughter of Ireland. Her faith in Jesus and her family and friends always took center stage.

She died on December 21 and her funeral was the day before Christmas Eve. The homilist remarked to the standing room only congregation that her death was such a gift to us. Who else could ever have convinced us to take a day out of shopping and hurried last minute preparations for Christmas? A day to slow down and remember the greatness of this God who was at the center of Vincent's life and to remember the enduring gift that her life was to all of us.

"You'll get my shillelagh when I am gone, Peg," she promised.

And her walking stick stands to this day in the corner by my front door and serves as a reminder to live in the present moment, to laugh at anger, to make happy memories. And most of all, to know that simplicity and humility are the true road to holiness. She taught many of us those lessons. I miss hearing her brogue, learning her lessons, sipping her tea. But I don't miss the essence of her because she is still here in all that she shared and all that she taught.

Saint Vincent de Paul II. She wouldn't like it. But the hearts that she touched would applaud and join in a hymn of praise to her. To get a seat, you would have to arrive very early.

Comfort Zone

I met Susan Hayward last week. No, not that Susan Hayward. She did not have the flowing red hair, ivory skin, or slim waist of the Hollywood icon. Or an Oscar proudly displayed in her home.

She was a thick woman. Strong body. Strong character. She had moved the year before from New York City to North Carolina. A lateral move professionally. From hospital aide to hotel chambermaid. She told me that she took a slight dip in pay but the rural setting and the riches of nature were well worth it.

In the luxurious setting of a five star hotel, the person that I bonded with was the woman who cleaned my room and made my bed. The bed with the pillow top mattress and down comforter, both of which you could order from the hotel catalog to be sent directly to your home for a "modest price." I felt out of place in the setting but comfortable with her. She was familiar. The stuff of common folk.

I was attending a professional conference as the guest of a participant. All expenses were paid and I was not obliged to attend any of the sessions.

The first morning, I snuck around the complex in my worn workout clothes on my way to the fitness room. After my workout, while others were at the seminar, I grabbed a gourmet takeout coffee and healthy muffin and headed back to my room for a shower. And there she was.

"I can come back later to do your room," she said.

"No need to do that," I answered.

She was just about to strip the bed and I told her to stop.

"Save the water," I told her. "I don't need clean sheets every day. Unless that would get you into trouble."

She assured me that it wouldn't.

I put the coffee and muffin aside. We made the bed together and I asked her to stop working.

"Sit down and take a break. I won't tell."

She did sit down and was grateful to be off of her feet for ten minutes. We lounged in leather chairs looking through floor to ceiling windows. The view held our focus while we chatted about things that were important to her. She told me that she was glad to have a job and to be out of the craziness of the city. Her kids loved looking at the mountains and liked their school where they easily made new friends. She never asked me about my family or where I worked. It seemed enough to be able to sit for a short while and tell me about things that made her proud.

There was no sense of demand in the room - verbal or non. Susan did not seem agitated or annoyed because I was in her work space. It didn't matter to me whether she worked or relaxed. We found ourselves in a tiny comfort zone bounded by a small room and a short time.

She had been working at the hotel for a year and was looking forward to her first weekend off - possible only after fifty-two weeks of service. Most of the time she was able to be there when her two young children got home from school. Sometimes her bus was late, though, so she was saving for a car. She did not like them to be alone.

I didn't ask her about who cared for her children as she worked the last fifty-two weekends and she did not offer the information.

We did the same the next day, Friday, and as Susan hugged me good-bye, I told her that there was one thing that I was sure was true.

"They don't pay you even close to what you're worth."

She smiled and thanked me for the envelope with the small tip. I told her that I would never see her again as I was certain that I would surely not pass this way in the future but that I was happy to meet her and to have the chance to chat.

Professionals from all over the country in their snazzy suits and designer shoes were everywhere in the hotel. There were bus drivers who shuttled us from site to site as we experienced the flavor of the South. Local tour guides were on each bus to give us a running narrative describing every neighborhood we rode through. We were treated to fine meals at elegant restaurants and local talent entertained us as we dined.

I experienced a slice of life during my four-day stay at the hotel. It occurred to me that Susan was part of the rind of that slice, rugged and hardy, and on the edge of society,

but keeping the slice from falling apart. My chambermaid.
A woman who enriched my life. Who taught me about
gratitude. And though I told her that, I am not sure she
believed me. Or heard me. She was on her way out the
door hurrying to the next room where unmade beds and
bathrooms in need of attention awaited her.

The Other Side of Middle Age

Emerging from middle age is grand. Some things are much easier. At the Y this morning there was a young woman on my left running at 6.5 MPH. (I peeked.) On my right was a young man running at 9.5 MPH. Wow. I was loping along at 3.0 knowing that it was just right. Working out is no longer motivated by cosmetics but rather by health. Increase bone mass. Lower blood pressure. Tighten up muscles. I was feeling good because I am able to walk at a good clip, on an incline, for 30 minutes before I do the weight machines. It's easy to let go of the frantic search for a perfect body. Emerging from middle age does that.

My internal voice has shifted. I pay more attention to my gut, to my wisdom, to my common sense and let others think what they will. It is knowing that if someone is mean it is more about them than it is about me. It gets easier with age and removes stress that doesn't ever need to be there.

Cells that were always task oriented have been reprogrammed. It's great to have a leisurely cup of coffee in the morning. Strong coffee that really is good to the last drop. I watch the birds and the squirrels as they do their thing outside my kitchen window. On warm days, coffee is on the front porch. With a watchful eye I guard the neighborhood.

There is time now to watch the next two family generations and to be in awe of the kids whose diapers I changed changing diapers of their own children. How they raise their babies with such care and tenderness. To watch their little ones as they discover life and beauty is such an enormous treat. To be able to stop at their homes to get a "kid fix." And then being able go back home with the scent of innocence and purity to carry me through a distressing day.

I can sort and toss and take the time to read every paper, card, letter and book that will not be returned to the shelf. It's ok to donate all the clothes in the "thinner" part of the closet not caring that I probably will never fit into them again. Old shoes gone. Old photos saved.

There is no guilt these days in working or reading or watching TV until 2:00 am and knowing that no alarm will need to be set for the morning. No rush to beat the traffic, to be on time, to be prepared for yet another work day. Naps are relished. Many days have Sabbath space with time to think, pray and wonder. There is a leisure here that is a welcome change.

The search for continued growth and development takes me down fresh paths. Paths that are personal and uncharted. It is a time when virtue takes on a different meaning. There is a new understanding of courage. A courage that is not focused on risking failure or taking on challenges but a courage that embraces new understandings without fear. There is an excitement for a generosity that rejects clutching things, time, or ideas close to me and embraces instead the experience of extending them to anyone who needs what I have to offer. Having takes a back seat to giving. It is when any duty can easily be set aside to make time for kindness. There is a modified sense of patience - to be able to just be, to be able to just listen, to be able to just wait.

The energy that was always present, allowing me to put in long days with plenty of overtime is gone. There is a new kind of energy now. An energy that gets me through the difficulties that present themselves, as these easy days do have some bumps in the road. Caring for a friend or relative in the hospital and witnessing pain while being helpless to ease it. Spending time at the nursing home and adjusting to the ravages of aging and illness. Crying freely at wakes and funerals. Working through all of the "whys" when preparing to say goodbye. And then, saying goodbye.

Understanding the rhythm of life is more of a priority now. But time is available to work at it. To put all that I have been taught into the mix in order to come up with answers that fit my experiences and stretch my faith. To reclaim in a new way beliefs that have sustained me through good days and bad.

I am grateful for all the days behind me that have formed me and prepared me for the future. In the meantime, I take each day as it comes enjoying the ease. Grief, when it happens, is the sweetest pain of all. It tells me about love never forgotten. Always present. Who could ask for anything more?

Drug Bust

Well. I happened upon a drug bust on my way to the hardware store. Third hardware store that I tried. First two were closed, since the giant depots have forced most of the little guys out of business. Couldn't open the front living room window until the screen was fixed. After yearning for warmth and fresh spring air during a long and cold winter, I was in a hurry.

A traffic light turned red and when I stopped I saw live drama on the corner. Two plain-clothes policemen had handcuffed a young troublemaker. The kid was dressed like a punk – underwear showing above his low-slung jeans. Baggy t-shirt. Jewelry everywhere. The police were searching every inch of his body. The search finished, they pushed his head down as he was getting into the unmarked car with the portable police light on the top. The traffic light turned green and as I drove away, I noticed a young woman standing nearby watching. She had been left alone during the arrest but she stayed. In place. Didn't move. Was the look on her face grief or fear or relief? Was she the girlfriend or a customer or an innocent by-stander?

The scene stayed in my head. The cops were dressed in dingy jeans and dirty t-shirts. The younger one had a baseball cap on backward. The other - no hat - salt and pepper hair trimmed military short. They were serious. The kid looked trapped, which he was.

He was young enough to have his father the same age as the cop with short hair. Would his father post bail? Or was he tired of rescuing his son? Or did his father even know who his son was, and what he was doing?

The kid had made a bad choice, obviously, and what would he do when he got out? For surely he was headed to a cell. Maybe he already knew his way around the inside. Maybe it was more home to him than home. I don't like that I judge like this. But I have had twenty years of watching my neighborhood decline and on some days the neighborhood itself dictates how I think about it.

I picked up the window screen and was stopped at the same traffic light on my way home. Everything was calm. No sign of any disturbance. The convenience store was still open and a guy was pumping gas at the corner station. The young girl was gone. With my car window down, I could hear the birds welcome spring. All seemed well as I headed home to put in the new screen. And to find the half broomstick I would need to prop the old window open.

You must understand that passing a drug bust on the way to anywhere is not that unusual in my neighborhood.

"Get out of there!" my friends urge.

How can I? I don't want to move. This neighborhood feels like home to me and it has shared stuff with me that no house with windows that work would ever see. For twenty years it has been a part of me. For twenty years I have been a part of it. Besides, we have a new landlord and he has promised to fix the place up. Maybe even put a shower in the bathroom. And get a new front door with a double lock.

But this is not about the window. Or the hardware. Or the drug bust. This is about the neighborhood where I live.

A young girl was strangled. Strangled in my neighborhood. No one knows the reason. A neighbor was stabbed to death on the street. Two young girls have disappeared without a clue. Houses have been boarded up but still display the scars of bullet holes. Drug transactions take place on the corners. My neighbors play loud music all weekend long making it impossible to sleep. Young men crazed with alcohol and drugs urinate in the street. Two police officers have been shot and killed in this neighborhood that needs help. Help that I am no longer able to give.

My friends are right. It is time to move. I can't hold on any longer. Comfort has turned to fear. I need to bid farewell to a neighborhood that no longer feels like home to me. That no longer has room for me.

Real life thugs have taken over the neighborhood. My neighborhood. Thugs who killed two police officers. Who strangled a young girl. Thugs who seem beyond reason. Beyond kindness. Thugs who make me afraid. Scare me enough to force me out of this place that has been home to me.

I wish I could stay, but I can't run as fast as I used to. I am not as strong as I used to be. Yes, I will have to leave. I wish I could stay. I wish I could help but I can't. I cannot help this neighborhood that has been home to me. This neighborhood that is no longer comfortable. This neighborhood that is deeply in need of salvation. This neighborhood where the cold winds of fear have found their way through the loose cracks in this old house.

A Giraffe Inside My Van
at the Drive Through Animal Park

The giraffe could have killed me and hurt herself. It would have been my fault. But, instead, I got my hand licked with her long purple/black tongue. I whispered into her ear as I stroked her broad and muscular neck. I tried to breathe as thinly as possible so that she would not detect a movement that could have signaled threat.

After a short time, I decided to usher the head and neck of this magnificent animal out of the front seat of my van the same way that she got in. I very slowly reached to my right as Rose handed me the bucket of animal food that I had given to her a few minutes before to feed the other giraffe outside of her window. The giraffe had come into the van in pursuit of the food that she had been enjoying outside my window. I moved the bucket an inch at a time while the giraffe continued to feed. She moved backward along with the bucket until they both were once again outside my window. It ended as it had begun. Peacefully and gracefully.

I can't stop thinking about this encounter. It left a mark of awe and gratitude on my spirit. And I wonder how the lesson from this giraffe could apply to other perceived threats. Strangely, I was not afraid, but at the same time I was aware that both Rose and I could be in danger. In danger because I took the bucket of food away so that the animal on the other side of the van could be fed. I took her food away. As soon as she made contact with the bucket again, she seemed satisfied. As she continued to feed, I strained to hear if she would purr. Nothing there. Just happy chomping.

Let me recap. There was a giraffe in my van. She seemed relaxed. Neither Rose nor I were in a panic. To any onlooker, it would have appeared that we were old pals and that the giraffe had come to the van for her regular afternoon feeding. There was a strange form of harmony going on. We had what she needed. She wanted it and we gave it to her. Happy ending. End of story. Or is it?

Was the happy ending because no harm was intended from either party? In a larger context, does it demonstrate that when you share what you have, others do not have to harm you or kill you to get what they need?

What would I do if someone threatened to take my food away if it were all I had with no chance of getting any more? I don't know. I just do not know what I would do. I am too blessed to even imagine it. What would any mother or father do if someone took away food meant for their children? What if everyone had enough to eat without fearing the theft of food, or home, or clothing. Or medicine?

How thinly would I breathe if there were a predator at my door? How thinly would I breathe if threats to my life and culture were real? How long could I hold my breath if gunmen were in the neighborhood? Or on my porch? I cannot imagine how I would breathe or not breathe. It has never happened to me. But it has happened. I read about it. I see it on the news. Bad things happen to good people. It happens to families. It happens to children. It often happens when people do not have what they need.

I treasure my experience with the giraffe. It put me skin close to a marvelous creature that I had no right to touch. That had no right being inside my van. But there she was. And there I was. And I want to learn something here because I believe that animals have so much to teach me. To teach all of us. They can't talk. But we can listen. And think. And observe. And wonder.

I fed the giraffe and she was content. What else, who else, is so skin close to me that I can reach out and touch? Touch with an intention that will lead to contentment. If I could touch and feed, if we all could touch and feed those who are hungry "What a Wonderful World" could become the new international anthem. Why not?

We can act with intention and will. Perhaps if everyone had the chance to hug a gentle giraffe's neck and to be soothed by a purple/black tongue the world would be a better place. With

> "trees of green. Skies of blue and clouds of white. With bright blessed days and dark sacred nights."

In the meantime, I must search for a way to translate that stunning moment into behavior that will help to feed and heal and serve. If there are enough people to work at it, we might someday be able to hear the whole world purr with contentment. As we watch "babies grow" and sing together, "what a wonderful world."

Mama Cass

I stood staring at the bay window with the curtain rod that was crooked. I just could not get the drapes to hang straight and I couldn't fix the rod. I made some calls for help. Some weren't home. The rest were too busy. I gave up on the drapes, sat down with some coffee and some music. And there she was. Singing.

"You gotta go where you wanna go
Do what you wanna do"

And then

"Monday, Monday, can't trust that day
Monday, Monday, sometimes it just turns out
that way"

I want to talk to Mama Cass. Since I can't call her on the phone, I'll be sure to look her up one day. Her voice soothes me but I don't know why. Maybe it's because I can hear her clear her throat before she starts to sing. That makes her seem a little more common than your usual star. Maybe it's because she was so overweight and was still a star that sang about sweet dreams and making your own kind of music. Maybe it's that honky tonk piano. No. It's the voice -- broad and warm and, oh, so friendly. She'd be fun on a trip and would include everyone present in the conversation. She'd say thanks for your help and tell you she could always depend on you. She'd leave a big tip for a hard working waitress and be here in a minute if you needed a hand with drapes that just won't hang right. But she's dead - heart attack in a London hotel. She died alone.

Maybe the people that didn't die can't sing like Mama Cass but they'll answer the phone and I know their number. They might be too busy to help with the drapes but they would leave a big tip and laugh at funny jokes.

Mama Cass is dead and I miss her. Especially now as I am feeling sorry for myself because I couldn't find anyone to help me with the stupid drapes.

It is a luxury feeling sorry for myself. Dangerous but a luxury just the same. Dangerous to become so self-centered. A luxury because I have time to do it. Time to feel sorry for myself.

I don't need to go to the river to carry water on my head back to some primitive hut. I don't have to glean someone else's field searching for grain to feed my family. I don't have to lie in fear during the night waiting for thugs to rip my house apart looking for someone that they perceive as an enemy of the state.

I don't have to be afraid to call Mama Cass to help me out and be afraid that she would say no. That she would, in a sense, reject me. I don't have to be afraid to call her because she is dead.

No. I just have to stand in my house and look at crooked drapes. Pitiful that I should feel sorry for myself because no one will come to help with the window treatments.

Or, I could go ahead and make my

"own kind of music,
sing my own special song, even if nobody else
sings along."

I could dance around the house and laugh at crooked drapes. I could give thanks for having a window to treat and a house to call home. I could give thanks for my blessings and make a promise to help someone who has way less than I do. Her music does that to me. So I will sashay out to the front porch and drink in some sunshine. To hell with curtains. All praise to Mama Cass for once again getting me out of a mood. I love all of those who were not home or were too busy to dash over to my living room. They were all doing something way more important than feeling sorry for themselves.

Mama Cass gave me

"sunshine on a cloudy day"

and I think I need to find a way to pass that on.

I never gave it a thought before, but maybe, just maybe, Mama Cass would like to talk to me.

Memories of Goodness

It is interesting to me how some memories of goodness are burrowed so deep in my being that they rarely surface. Memories of days gone by stored on some mental or emotional shelf. Then in an instant, something or someone pops one to the surface. It happened today. It was a letter that did it. A letter that brought a long moment of joy.

She was my friend. She moved away and I lost touch. It happens. For thirty-four years she was on some shelf. Then, up she popped today.

How does a person process year after year of hellos, and then good-byes? Only a few stay for the long haul. But each real hello and each real good-bye makes an impact. There is no such thing as no more room in my mind or in my heart or in my memory for the experience of love or kindness or generosity from kindred spirits.

I share what I have and who I am with those given to me during the now moment and they share with me in return. It is a nourishing and a rich experience, made more compelling, perhaps, by the sharing and nourishing that has gone before and that has brought me to the present. How do I put them all together in order to see who I have become because of the presence of goodness in my life?

Maybe there is no need for more. Today was sweet. It was total. It was enough.

A Root Beer Mentor

She was a sturdy woman. Short and thick. From head to toe. She frightened me with her dour face and gruff manner. Later I would find out that she was in constant pain. I was green then and had not yet learned the lessons that she would teach me with her words. With her life. With her friendship.

She became my mentor and I learned to treasure her. Years later when she was bedridden, I took her root beer when I visited. Ice cold root beer.

She had time then. And I would spend hours at her bedside talking to her, trying to soak up as much wisdom as I could.

She was born February 9, 1904 in a small Pennsylvania town and was christened Gertrude Reedy on February 21, 1904. As a young woman, she entered the Sisters of the Humility of Mary on December 8, 1925, and chose Sister Mary David as her religious name. Perhaps the study of her patron, the boy wonder who later became king of all of the Israelites, added to her native wisdom. David, the courageous lad who slew Goliath, later had a major fall from grace. He faced his sins, sought forgiveness, picked himself up, and went on to become a kind and generous ruler.

Study him she did, and incorporated the lessons of his life into hers. And she shared many of them with me.

Mary David would challenge me as no one else ever had. I could get away with nothing. She did it because she cared for me and I knew it. As I sat at her bedside, I grew up. She taught me to own my behavior and to put blame for it where it belonged.

"You made the choice," she would say, "so now you really have to live with it. You did it to yourself, and you have no one else to blame."

Then we would dissect together what I had done or not done. We would try to pinpoint motives so that I could free myself from that kind of behavior. She was better at it than I was, so I tried to pay close attention. Our times together were truly sacramental. They were moments filled with grace. Moments filled with grace over a shared ice cold root beer.

Mary David was a professional. A nurse and a teacher, she knew her work and she practiced it with efficiency and with deep compassion, even while living with pain the final years before she became bedridden.

Yes, she was gruff but her heart was soft and generous. She took a special interest in her students and protected them from the ones who weren't gruff. Ones who were sweet and all smiles. Who when annoyed had sharp tongues and mean hearts.

"Pay them no mind," she would say. "They are just unhappy people who will try to take it out on you. Don't let them. Just don't let them upset you. Their meanness is about them, not about you. Don't let them frighten you."

The day that we lost Mary David in 1982 was the day that she lost her pain. She was ready. She had yearned for eternal peace for a long, long time. She was gone, but she did not take with her the wisdom that she had shared with so many of us:

- Don't be fooled by those with serene faces and mean hearts.
- Accept responsibility for your decisions, good or bad.
- Give gruff people a chance to share their goodness.
- Your compassionate behavior will bless you.
- Extraordinary lessons are just around the corner.
- People who really care for you will always tell you the truth no matter how hard it is to hear.
- Face yourself with honesty.
- Admit your mistakes and resolve to do better the next time.
- Your heart matters more than your face.
- Don't forget that delivering a cold drink can be the most soothing moment in an otherwise painful day.

So here's to you, Mary David. I toast you as I think of you today. I toast you with an ice cold root beer. I relish its refreshment as I relish enduring memories of time spent with you. Thank you, dear friend, thank you. Thank you for timeless lessons. Thank you for a soft and generous heart. Thank you for never giving up on those of us who loved you. We still do. We still love you. And, thanks be to God, we know that you continue to love us as well from your place of eternal, pain free rest.

Melancholy

I have in me a pocket of melancholy. A big pocket. A bubble with infinite boundaries that grow at will. Packed with some regrets. Dreams not chased. Memories of what ifs. Youthful ideals. People grown old. Days gone by. Of war and rice paddies. Of soldiers dead.

It is filled with peace marches, with boycotts, with friends no longer here, with music of the 60s, with the horror of assassinations, with raisins in the sun. With secrets of my heart.

There are blind spots, too, in this wistful bubble, and also some chilling moments. But each time I take a look, the view becomes more and more interesting. Years of living with new understandings and new meanings overlay the memories and bring some new perspectives. But there is not a lot that I would change.

Even though I do not long for yesterday, I do like to visit that bubble once in a while. Some of the memories re-energize me for today. For tomorrow. I visit the bubble to sing the songs that formed my soul. To plead for growth. To sing new songs. And to remind myself that in some cases change and newness came from tiny steps. Women suffragettes. The voice of a young Southern minister. A woman who would not move to the back of the bus. An old man named Roncalli. The fasting of a California farm worker. The fall of the Berlin Wall. The end of apartheid. The election of an African American President.

I visited that bubble today because I listened to Joan Baez. (I sang.) I re-read Catcher in the Rye. (I smiled.) I watched the memorial service from Fort Hood. (I wept.)

I gave thanks for being there in those days. For being here in these days. For knowing that the times are still a changin'. I gave thanks for what is not yet realized but still possible.

This left-over empire of my mind that grabbed hold of every glory and every defeat and every possibility is perhaps tinged with a little fiction. Retrospection often does that. But I am glad I made the trip today. I still enjoy the view.

And I emerged with a new hope for energy to keep on truckin'. To still sing, to still smile, to still weep. To still plead for world peace. For the energy to do my little part in trying to make this world a better place.

One tiny, tiny step at a time.

Born to Die

"For the world's more full of weeping than you can understand."*

We are born to die. That's the truth. And I find myself obsessing about it these days. So many are sick. And dying. So many wakes. Funerals. Bereavement dinners. I want it to stop. But the truth is we are born to die.

Denial runs very high in my mind. No, it won't happen. Then it does. Who's next? It will never be me. Who can ever imagine that? Imagine one's own death?

Better to live in the moment and just take a day at a time. Conventional wisdom. Doesn't really help much. Not today. My heart aches today.

But what about my clutter? Should I clean out now or leave it for someone else to sort? Who gets what? Should I decide or not? AAAARRRAUGH! I feel so Charlie Brownish today.

Leave these thoughts and go to gratitude. Immediately. Go to gratitude immediately.

I want to insulate myself from death. Yet everyday, first thing, I read the obituaries in the morning newspaper. Reality staring me in the face.

There are wonders, too.

Leave these thoughts and go to gratitude. Immediately. Go to gratitude immediately.

O.K.

I am grateful for life. Short or long. I am grateful for family and friends. Companions on the journey. I am also grateful for the journey itself. For models of devotion. For love and tenderness. Beauty lifts my spirit and fills my soul. Music takes me to a glorious space. Children's laughter makes me giddy. I could gaze forever at the stars and moon on a clear night. The warmth of the sun takes the chill off of any fear. The words of poets and the work of artists inspire me. I so enjoy fields of daffodils. The roar of the ocean. The whisper of the wind. Soft cooling rain.

Every day I read the obituaries. First thing.

I tell myself to stop obsessing. Drink in the universe. Open myself to love, warmth and beauty. This is what is now, in this moment, gift, treasure and grace.

So, yes. Sickness, funerals, bereavement dinners. But also births, baptisms, First Communions, weddings. Heartache and joy. They seem to balance. Age wise being somewhere between the two is not a bad place to be in life. So I will hold close the tears and the gladness. Keep my clutter. Walk in the rain. Sit in the sun. Love and be loved.

I will mourn loss. I will celebrate life.

I will hold on to wonder and recognize that love is the root of grief.

I will embrace the journey through joy. I will endure the journey through sorrow.

And check you-know-what in tomorrow morning's newspaper. First thing.

*The Stolen Child, William Butler Yeats

Strangers in
a Strange Land

A *Kirundi Hymn*

I heard the warmest of sounds and the sweetest of all Christmas offerings. The melody told me that it was O Come All Ye Faithful but I did not understand a word of his native Kirundi language. This eighteen-year-old refugee man/child was sitting next to me as I drove him home from the Catholic Charities Christmas party for refugee families. Once in the car, he began to sing, and I could have driven for miles in order to hear his gift to me. The drive did not last forever. Only the five minutes it took for me to get him and his two little sisters home from the party. Only the length of one glorious hymn.

None of them spoke or understood a word of English. But on this night, we all understood the universal language of music. And dance. At their request, the families had danced for us to end the evening festivities.

I had gone to a meeting six weeks before, to learn about the refugee families coming into our city and the need for mentors to help them through the initial weeks of intrigue and uncertainty as they settled into their new homes. They had left terror behind when they fled their country of Burundi for the refugee camp in Tanzania.

I volunteered to be a family mentor. The family that I was to work with was Hutu; they had escaped the oppression of the Tutsi gangs in their homeland. The next week, I paid them a visit with two other mentors and an interpreter. Grandmother, mother, father, and five children had recently been settled into a modest duplex in a poor area near my city.

They were gracious and welcoming people as we sat in their simple new home and learned about them, and them about us, while a fellow countryman of theirs interpreted our conversation. But we did not need an interpreter to understand their happiness in being free and safe.

Burundi is one of the world's poorest nations and has been plagued by civil war and tension between the Tutsi minority and the Hutu majority for many years. This family did not need to worry about that ever again.

Just before we left, the interpreter asked the dad what he needed. We were told that what he said was boots for his children. I sent an email to twenty generous friends when I got home that evening and in one week I had enough money to get boots and gloves for the parents, the grandmother, and all five children, with some money left over for the next need. Catholic Charities had provided winter coats, and another donor had given hats and scarves for this family who had never been cold or seen snow.

This Burundi family reminded me of another family who had traveled far on the first Christmas. There was no bright star in the sky the night we visited our new friends. No angels singing. No shepherds or royalty. But the simplicity was the same. The poverty was similar. And the generosity of twenty people was as valuable to them, I believe, as gold, frankincense, or myrrh.

I dropped the children off after the Christmas party and hummed O Come All Ye Faithful all the way home. No words. Just humming. I did not want to spoil the memory or the experience with English words. Next year, I resolve to sing along in Kirundi.

Penina

Anyone who really knows me knows that I don't sing or dance. I can do a lot of things. But sing and dance? No. Until Penina sees me coming. With her arms wide open in greeting, she sways and sashays towards me in a most elegant manner. What am I to do? Of course I sway and sashay right into her arms in response. Not elegant, I admit. But it feels so good to return her greeting in that way.

Penina is a grandmother who fled with her family from Burundi to safety in a refugee camp in Tanzania. Through the United Nations, the U.S. State Department and Catholic Charities, she was resettled with her family in Cleveland, Ohio. I was most fortunate to be assigned as a mentor to her family that included her daughter and son-in-law and their five children. This family has blessed me with their courage and their warmth. With their trust and their friendship.

So it took no thought or effort on my part to take off my socks on a chilly, rainy fall day so that Penina's feet that were so used to African warmth would no longer be bare. Her eleven-year-old grandson translated for her yesterday when I visited. "She wants to know if you will get her some socks," he said to me. I will take her a full pack of new socks tomorrow, but for now her feet are warm.

She speaks so fast to me in Kirundi as though I understand every word. I don't understand any of her words but her gestures are another matter. A groan and a hand on her knee tell me that her arthritis is acting up. She needs some Advil. An open mouth and a whimper let me know that she needs to go to the dentist. A sway and a sashay tell me that she is glad to see me. She holds out a portion of cooked corn meal and points. I take the offering, dip it into the tasty gravy and smile my appreciation for her native cuisine. We talk to each other all of the time that way, sharing the universal language of welcome and friendship.

She carries a white plastic purse whenever she leaves the house. Her papers that tell where she came from and why she is here are the only contents. She is proud of those papers. I can tell by the way she carries the purse. By the way she holds it open so I can get a glimpse of the treasures that are hers.

Sometimes I think of my own immigrant grandmother when I see her. They do not seem to be much alike, but in the long run, I guess there is not much difference between corned beef and goat meat. Not much difference in gratitude for a new home. Not much difference in the homesick moments when families from far away are missed with a certain, deep longing. Although my grandma did not dance either, I suppose there is not much difference between sashaying into a warm Burundi embrace and leaning into a good old Irish hug.

Sharing a meal, a little dance now and then, a warm welcome, sharing what you have with a generous spirit – this is the language I share with Penina. A universal language. A warm language. A language of the heart.

And by the way, I would gladly trade a pair of socks for a bit of corn meal dipped in tasty gravy any day of the week. More than a bargain. A reminder of friendship that is pure gift. Thank you, Penina. Thank you, my friend.

Pim Si

There are five children – 4 girls and one boy. Pim Si is the youngest and she is the one who pays the least attention to me. She is two years old.

The waiting room in the hospital lab was filled with children and their parents from her country who had shared life in a refugee camp in Thailand. They had fled their homes in Burma to escape persecution and terror. I sat and visited with the interpreter while Pim Si went with her mother, Shee Nay, into the exam room to have blood drawn. The lab technicians were testing all of the children for lead levels. I could hear Pim Si crying and screaming and thought about going in to be with them but decided that it was more appropriate for me to stay in the waiting area. In retrospect, I should have gone in.

On the ride home, Shee Nay asked if I had heard Pim Si crying. I assured her that I had.

"Did you hear her call your name?" she asked. "She kept calling, 'Peg, Peg, Peg!' "

I had not heard her call my name. It did surprise me though because, after all, she is the child who pays the least attention to me. But the thought of it is wrapped around my heart. It has carried me on a wave of delight and gratitude. I felt drawn even closer to this family that I have come to love.

My volunteer commitment time as a family mentor has long expired. When I told Shee Nay that I was proud of how well they had settled in their new home, their new city, their new country, she seemed pleased. Until I told her that it was time for me to move on, because she and her husband had learned enough to be able to be on their own. I would still be her friend, but no longer a mentor.

"No, no," she said. "We need you."

They don't. The truth of the matter is that I need them.

Visiting them is the favorite part of my day. Serving them enriches my life. Knowing them expands my world. Loving them warms my heart. Being with them helps me to better know who I am. The truth of the matter is that I need them.

I do: I drive the parents. I tutor the children. I talk to welfare officers and school officials. To doctors and city officers. I teach bus routes to Shee Nay and to her husband Heh Si and give tips for the unfamiliar reality of winter. I go to school concerts and hospital emergency rooms. I shop with Shee Nay and slowly read labels in grocery stores and pharmacies. I explain water bills and thermostats. I take a pizza now and then and a small gift on birthdays.

They give: They welcome me into their home. They give me their trust; I am the one that they call when there is something they don't understand or when they have a specific need. They demonstrate their affection with hugs and hospitality. They share their culture and their food. They sing for me and dance. They radiate gratitude with thank you after thank you. Shee Nay, Heh Si, and their five children embody goodness and humility in their simplicity and authenticity.

They fill me up to overflowing.

They show me the face of God.

Home

Gettysburg Address

I was scared nearly to death and I wanted to stay home from school. My mother wisely told me it would be best to go and not put the trial by fire off for one more day.

"Go," she said, "and raise your hand to be the first."

Her advice became tattooed on my psyche. Her words to me became a defining moment.

So I did what she said. I raised my hand to be first and then I recited the whole Gettysburg Address in good time and with no mistakes. I secretly hoped when I sat down that I would someday be as smart as my mother.

I had escaped the wrath of my seventh grade teacher

who struck fear in all of our hearts. On a daily basis. I secretly hoped when I sat down that I would never be as mean to people as she was to us. I didn't know why she was so mean. It was beyond me to try to figure it out. All of my energy in that classroom was dedicated to avoiding her temper.

My guess now is that she just did not like kids. Or that she wanted to be somewhere else and not in a seventh grade classroom. I will never know. Never know why she came to school everyday with an anger that we did not deserve.

I didn't know as a seventh grader that my mother suffered from my anxiety, too. She would have done almost anything to protect me from the wrath of my teacher. Almost anything except let me stay home from school. She would protect me when she could but she would not keep me from learning important life lessons. She was at the door when I came home and I still remember her happy hug.

I wonder now about other moments. Certainly life has not been dominated by fear but some of those memories are the sharpest that I have. I think of those times that I wouldn't let go and chose to be afraid instead. What is it that sometimes gives the fear more power in our lives than the love?

I suspect everyone has a Gettysburg Address story. I hope everyone with their stories were blessed as well with a source of wisdom. A voice that said you can do it. Do it now. And then it will be finished.

I am no longer that seventh grader. She lived in the last millennium. What I have found out since then is that I can face fear and stare it down. Not easy but do-able. I just need to remember the joy of my mother when I walked through that door after school. It warms me to this day. I need to remember that tattoo on my psyche. To remember her faith in me. To know that life can be tough but so can I. Face the fear and it is soon over. Put it off and it lasts and lasts.

I miss my mother. Her loss still saddens me. But her lessons are so deep that they are beyond erosion. And so are those words of Abraham Lincoln:

"Four score and seven years ago. . . ."

In a way I am grateful for that teacher, too. If it had not been for her, I would not have had the opportunity to overcome what was a major step in my young life. I would have preferred kindness. But what kindness I really needed was waiting for me at home. It was freely given and freely received. And it was enough.

My Uncle Matt

Horace was a Latin lyric poet who lived more than two millennia ago. In the Epilogue from his third book of Odes he wrote,

"I have erected a monument more lasting
than bronze
And taller than the regal peak of pyramids.
I shall never completely die."

I read that quote in the newspaper the other day. That's what he said. I shall never completely die. Although he was referring to his poetry, cannot each of us hope to say the same about our life and the lives of the ones we love? Even about the ones we know about but never really got the chance to know? Can a life be a monument more lasting than bronze? Only if remembered? Who will remember? Which life, besides Horace's, will never completely die?

Did you ever walk down a crowded street looking at hundreds of people, hundreds of faces that you will never see again? Did you ever stop at a traffic light and catch a glimpse of the driver in the next car, in all probability, never to be seen again? Do you ever think about these once in a lifetime encounters? I do. We will never run out of people that we do not know.

So if there are literally billions of people that we will never know, is it too much to ask that we actively remember the ones that are directly connected to us, even if we never met them in person?

I used to have an Uncle Matt. Well, technically I didn't. He died before I was born. But if he had lived longer or if I had been born earlier, I would have really had an Uncle Matt.

I was thinking the other day that there is no one left to remember him. No one to remember my Uncle Matt. All who knew him are dead. I know a little about him but I did not know him. So I wonder if my thinking about him and the fact that I know his name and have his photo means that he is still remembered. And how do I pass that on and on and on? For some reasons that I do not understand, I feel that it is my responsibility to do so.

Uncle Matt was twenty-one when he had a seizure in Church and he died soon after. My grandmother never really got over it.

My mother told me a little about her oldest brother. He was, mostly, ordinary. But greatly loved, and I have this strange need to make sure that this uncle that I never knew personally is remembered. By someone.

Here's what I know. He was born of an Irish mother and an English father in Durham County, England. He sailed from Southampton with his family when he was eight years old. I have a copy of the ship manifest. Matthew's occupation is listed as scholar because he was in the third grade when they left their home. They arrived in New York on the Aquatania in October, 1920.

"Not in steerage." my mother would say.

That was an important fact that we should never forget. We should never forget that they did not come as paupers.

Uncle Matt's passport photo is framed and on my photo shelf.

My grandfather, grandmother, their two sons and daughter settled in a small coal-mining town in Pennsylvania. They were church going people. Roman

Catholic. And then Matt was here and gone. One day. In Church. Here one moment and gone the next. My grandfather stopped going to church the day his son died. The day Matt died in church.

They never talked much about him – the ones who knew and loved him. Perhaps their grief was still too present. Still too raw to touch. I wish now that I had asked more about him.

Before my youngest brother's first child was born, our mother asked him if he would consider the name Matthew if the baby were a boy.

My youngest brother called her from the hospital the day of the birth.

"It's a boy." he said. "We named him Matthew. We named him for your brother."

My mother wept.

In the final analysis, this is not only about Uncle Matt. This is about the brevity of our lives. This is about what small worlds most of us live in. Here one day. Gone the next. So what do we do in between? In between here and gone. We may as well be happy and generous. Deal with setbacks and heartbreak. What else is there?

Once gone, what do we leave behind? Where is our mark? Who will remember and why? How important is it to be remembered? Remembered longer than the lives of those who knew us personally.

The real answers to these questions may rest somewhere beyond words. In the meantime, this is for you Uncle Matt. I remember you and I will pass you on to the next generation. I hope they will do the same so that you shall never completely die. My duty done, I can one day rest in peace. And finally, leave all of the remembering to others.

Common Grace

She was the most common of common women. She was, literally, an Irish washerwoman with the soul of an angel. Dead 39 years, I did not know how much I still missed her until last week when she was so alive and warm in my dream.

"I have a message for you," she said.

"What is it, Grandma?" I asked.

"I will tell you on Tuesday," she replied.

Well, Tuesday came and went and no message that I could see. Or hear. Except that I could not stop thinking about her. Maybe that was the message. Take some time to remember and maybe to learn.

Grandma never wanted to go back to Ireland. Life was harsh for her there. Taken out of school after the second grade, she went to work at a rich neighbor's farmhouse to help her family. Her father was an army pensioner, her mother a domestic for a wealthy English family living in County Kilkenny with more power and influence than any of the poor Irish families who were their neighbors.

At eighteen she left home with her younger sister and older brother to find work in a small town in England. It was there that she was employed at the local college laundry. A handsome young gentleman, a meat cutter, was smitten with her. They married and had three children. In 1920, age thirty-five, she sailed for New York with her husband and children. She never looked back. Never.

She was the most common of common women. Having experienced harshness in her youth, she was determined to leave it behind when she set sail. She yearned only to be close to her family. As the family grew, we became her new world. We were her riches, her fortune. And we worshipped at her knee. She taught us the value of being loving and kind and generous. Not much else mattered.

Her first granddaughter, I share her name. After my grandfather died, she moved in with us and she was my roommate for four years. And today, 39 years since she died,

I miss her presence in my life. But then, there is that dream. She is with me still. I have no idea what that means. I cannot understand it. But I sense it. I believe it.

So I am spending time relishing memories of my grandmother and of her most generous heart. She made all of us feel that we were God's greatest creation. And a gift to her.

How beautiful to be common. How grace-filled and noble it can be. Common ripples through our lives and makes the world go around. Common builds bridges and tills the land. Common is our next door neighbor who helps in a pinch. A kind cashier when grief overwhelms us. The cop who patrols our neighborhood. The teacher who believes in us. Common is a mother who weeps when her child is treated unfairly. A dad who plasters and paints his kid's first home. Common is life for most of us. Common is what teaches us what it means to be human. And, perhaps, a little bit divine.

What a pleasure it is to set aside time to give thanks for the saints among us – past and present. It gives me joy and fills me with gratitude. My grandma, all these years later, is somehow with me. I still cannot understand it. So I rely instead on memories of a warm hug, eyes that twinkle, a great Sunday dinner. A dollar slipped into my pocket. The memory of being loved beyond measure.

So that was her message.

Received and understood. Thank you.

Hope Around the Corner

We were going to the County Department of Job and Family Services to find out what kind of health benefits were due my ailing mother. We had an appointment: 8:30 a.m.

My sister-in-law, Joyce, and I were not going to take any chances so we arrived at 8:10 a.m. We were greeted by an older woman in slacks and a flowered smock buttoned all the way to her neck. She directed us to window #2 - the window for those with appointments. There was no line. The No Appointments Window #3 already had a long line. The clerk at our window reached for our paper work and told us to have a seat. We did. It was a cavernous room set up with metal folding chairs. We sat and faced a glass-enclosed office where an armed policeman stood and scanned the room. It was, evidently, his only job. Unless, of course, some one got tired of waiting, waiting, waiting and made some trouble. Joyce and I were strangers in a strange land.

We sat in silence as did all but three of those waiting. They turned their chairs and chatted with each other in a low tone. Another woman was reading a book. A young man, late teens, was sitting beside his young son trying to keep the kid from making a fuss. Another young man walked in, carrying an infant in a baby seat. He scanned the crowd before he took a seat. All races. All ages. Both genders. We sat obediently and waited.

A woman popped open the door and called my name. It was 8:35. People who had arrived before we did watched as we left our seats and headed for the door. (We did have an appointment.) We followed the woman down a long stretch passing cubicle after cubicle until she made a turn into hers. I introduced her to Joyce but she didn't seem interested. She never told us her name but her name plate did: SuAnne. She sat behind her desk in the small cubicle, drank a long drink of water from her designer bottle, and then started to type. It was then that I noticed her manicured fingernails - long, with bright red polish sprinkled with gold glitter.

We sat and watched.

"Do you have the information that you were told to bring," she asked, looking at us for the first time.

I gave her the folder - thick with documentation that had taken me days to gather. More typing.

"You are missing five pieces of information," she said.

She handed me a check list with the items that I still needed to provide. More typing. Joyce and I were both just sitting there. I was in another zone somewhere when, suddenly, she yelled,

"Route 77 really isn't that bad, Darlene. Both lanes are still open. You just have to shift a little bit. I just got back from vacation."

In the middle of her comments to Darlene, I realized that she was talking to the woman in the next cubicle. She was more in tune with the woman on the other side of the six foot high wall that she was with us. The sudden comment about Route 77 startled me. I was in a stupor, after all.

More typing. Another swallow from her water bottle. I noticed a full sized poster that she had on the side of her metal filing cabinet:

*"Everything I ever needed to know,
I learned in kindergarten."*

The magnets holding the poster were an advertisement for Prozac. It amused me and I wondered if the Prozac would be more appropriate for the woman typing, or for the two of us sitting, waiting for the next question, or for the next reprimand we would get for forgetting something.

She had made no human contact with us and it was clear that our job was to sit and to speak only when she spoke to us. It was machine like and uncomfortable. I wondered if the same thing were going on in those many cubicles that we had passed on our way to her desk.

"That's it. It looks as if your mother will qualify," she said. "As soon as you get me the missing information the process will be completed. You won't have to come back. I will give you an envelope to mail the missing data."

We stood as she did and thanked her for her time and service. During the nearly two hours that we answered questions and watched her type, there was not one qualitative human exchange. On the way out, I looked back and told her I had one question.

"I am fascinated by the orange on your desk." I said.

A human being answered.

"Oh, that," she replied. "I forgot and left an orange on my desk one Friday and when I came back on Monday it was dried out. I keep telling them that the air is too dry in here and we need some kind of humidifier. How can an orange dry out in one weekend?"

"Just wondered about it," I said, as we followed her back down the corridor, and through the door back into the room filled with metal chairs where people who had no appointments still waited to be called.

I wondered if they, too, were drying out in air that so needed a humidifier.

We talked on the way home about the time and the concentration that it took to gather the info for the folder - and that it still wasn't right. We questioned whether people who could not read or write or understand English very well could navigate this system. Did they know to make an appointment? What would have been missing from their pockets or envelopes or perhaps, an occasional folder? We talked about how long they would have to sit in that cavernous room before they were called. How long they would sit in a cubicle before they were told to go home and get the information that was missing.

We never asked. We did not want to take any chances. We waited until were safe in our mini-van on the way home to talk about it.

I called my brother when I got home to report our experience.

"I feel so sorry for SuAnne," he said. "Can you imagine a full day of gathering data, data and more data with no time to connect on a personal level?"

His statement knocked me off my judgment and I was ashamed. While I was busy being insulted by robotic behavior, SuAnne was busy doing her job. Doing her job efficiently. Her lack of chatting and personal interaction shaved minutes off of our interview. Those minutes, along with the ones she shaved off of other appointments perhaps gave her time to see one or two additional people during her busy day. One or two others who had the knots in their stomachs dissolved as she turned from her computer to tell them that "you will qualify for assistance."

So thank you lady with the dried orange on your desk and with red glittered fingernails. Thank you for ignoring me and doing your job. And by the way, my mother is doing well.

The Eighth Sacrament

I am convinced that care giving is the eighth sacrament. Yes, a sacrament. Definitely a sacrament. An outward sign (and I am not sure about this but I would bet my bottom dollar on it) instituted by Christ. Christ, care giver deluxe. An outward sign, instituted by Christ to give grace. Grace to do what I am not cut out to do.

It started as a two day trip to take my dad to his doctor for a routine check up and to celebrate his birthday the second day. It ended in twelve days caring for him after emergency surgery for a detached retina. We learned of the need for surgery on his birthday. His eighty-ninth birthday. He told me, when he was diagnosed with bladder cancer eleven years earlier, not to worry about him because he was a "tough old guy" and that he would beat the cancer. He did. We had the birthday party for this tough old guy the night before surgery and he had a grand time.

Three days after surgery: shingles. I got him to the doctor immediately and the pain was somewhat controlled by the medication.

An outward sign instituted by Christ to give grace. Grace to cleanse a broken eye. To keep his hands away from painful shingles. To do what I am told. And I was told what to do every nano second. Check the back door a million times a day to make sure it is locked. Close the drapes. Pick a paper off the kitchen floor. Get the salt and pepper on demand. Heat up his warm coffee. Turn out that light. To make sure he put on clean socks and underwear every day. To watch for signs of physical weakness. I was given the grace to sleep on the couch so that I could answer his bell several times a night so that he didn't fall on his way to the bathroom. To make sure that he looked at the floor eight days straight to keep the gas bubble in his eye in place long enough for the retina to heal. To answer to my mother's name every time he called me.

I bought him a pound of shrimp - big shrimp, huge shrimp - the last night I was there because, as his granddaughter told him, he had been a brave little soldier. Well, I am finally home where people that I know call me by my own name.

Through all of his demands for total attention and servitude, he was grateful for my presence. His trust in my ability was total. Misplaced, perhaps, but total.

This was not my first experience in care giving. What I learned early on is that the role is not to be a helper for someone who is ill. Not to look upon the patient as being in a lesser state. To understand that those I serve are those who serve me as well. Who teach me about the importance of presence. The importance of compassion. Who give me the opportunity to go beyond myself no matter how difficult the struggle. To live with my impatience and irritation and to know that I will have another opportunity very soon to be patient and kind. Who give me the strength not to blow every chance. Because they believe that I can do it. That I will do it. They believe that I care. And I do.

I am beyond exhaustion but grateful for the privilege. Could it be that this is what we were created to do? Could this be the washing of the feet that we were taught? Could this be the great opportunity to love one another? Could this be the opportunity to be the most human that we can be? To lay down our time, our energy, our care, for one another? To do what we have no confidence in doing? For our dad? For our mom? Brother or sister? Friend? For all of those who have their names carved on the palm of God's hand?

If all of life is a circle, perhaps care giving is one very important entry point. There will come a day when someone will need to make sure that I have clean underwear. That I smell good. That I don't fall. That I get my meds on time. Hopefully, that person will be kind and patient and will be grateful for the opportunity to be of service. And in that person's future, there will be another care giver who will do the same. Who will understand the eighth sacrament and embrace the grace that goes with it.

Bradley's Gift

I cradled that dog's head in my arms and sobbed as I told him what a good dog he had been. I told him that he had brought such deep joy to an old man and his wife both of whom treasured every day of his presence. As I thanked him for the goodness he was, I told him not to be afraid because he would be o.k. and that his legs would not hurt anymore. Not to worry. A human person. Had I neared a moment of insanity as I talked to that dog as though he were a person? A human being. Was I talking to him as if I thought he understood my every word?

I held him until the injection did its work. Then he was gone. He was a Golden Retriever. Zack was his name.

The grief that followed the loss of such a faithful companion was deep and real.

"No more dogs," my dad said. "I would only have a Golden Retriever and in six months, a new puppy would be big enough and frisky enough to knock your mother over. So no more dogs. That's final."

I got a phone call a few months later.

"There's a dog I want you to go and see. A Golden Retriever waiting to be adopted. Six years old. The friskiness will be calmed down. This might be the one."

I saw the dog and indeed he was the one. Trained, calm and gentle. He offered his paw as I greeted him and sat quietly as I petted him. I could have sworn he was smiling. Bradley was his name. No second thoughts. I took him to my mother and dad the same day I first saw him. When we went into the house, the dog went straight to my mother's chair, sat and put his paw on her knee. For seven years, he never left their sides.

As my mother aged, she began to fail. There came a moment when the family realized that we could no longer give her what she needed at home. With broken hearts we made the decision to have her move into a nursing facility that could give her competent and tender care. My dad visited her every day and often took Bradley with him.

Dad started to slow down but refused to give up driving. We tried to figure out a way to convince him to go into assisted living in the same complex where my mother resided. We tried every angle. He would only have to walk down the hall to visit his wife and all of his meals would be prepared for him. Good food and good company would be just outside his door. The catch was that we knew the eighty-five pound dog was too big for assisted living and the truth was that he would never part with his pal.

One day my dad called my brother Tom at work to tell him that he thought Bradley had died during the night. Tom raced to the house. My dad was lying on the floor next to Bradley sobbing and petting his beloved dog. Tom told me that he, too, broke down and that it was one of the saddest things that he had ever seen.

Soon after, my dad had a major medical emergency. He was in the hospital for two weeks and went to the nursing home when he was released to continue his physical therapy. He never returned to his home. He went from the nursing home therapy wing to assisted living. And, yes, just down the hall. That could never have happened if Bradley had not died.

What was sadness for all of us became Bradley's gift to him. Calm and gentle indeed.

Is it too far out to think that my mother and dad are in some smooth green field cavorting these days with Zack and Bradley? Perhaps it is. But nobody knows for sure. I admit it does make a lovely tale. A comforting image for those of us who love animals. And perhaps a great truth. I guess that I will just have to wait and see. And maybe I will find a pocket to tuck in a rawhide bone when I make my trek to the other side.

Just in case.

Beauty, Deep Beauty

"I have loved you for so long," she whispered to me from the couch where she was resting. I sat by her side as she stroked my cheek. About to leave for home after a weekend of shared care giving, I felt sad as she weakened physically and began to show signs of memory loss and confusion. That happened almost three years ago but the energy, love and intensity of that moment has lifted me beyond sadness and created a pillow of comfort and gratitude that I rely on to this moment.

My mother died today. As I experienced overwhelming grief at the loss of a true-life companion, I realized in a guilt filled way that I was deeply relieved as well. For her. She had suffered for almost three years from a debilitating form of dementia. Her beauty was deep: skin deep, heart deep and soul deep. She always took pride in how she looked and how she took care of herself. She loved without reserve. She was filled with faith and hope. Her illness stripped so much away that she did not seem to be the mother that I had treasured all of my life. But she was. Still. And forever.

Having five brothers and an alpha male father drove us together early. We did girl things. We cleaned and cooked. We shopped. Enjoyed musical theater. Planned, bought and wrapped gifts. Shared books and magazines. We found pockets of time and sacred spaces to escape the testosterone filled atmosphere.

Despite the guys, she created a home filled with kindness and warmth. All were welcome and many responded to her hospitality and generosity. Always ready for a good conversation, we talked, debated, agreed, disagreed with anyone who stopped in for a visit and a cup of coffee or a game of cards.

She had been a budding writer who won a trip to a college summer workshop in writing with an essay she wrote as a teenager. Not bad for a young girl from a tiny Pennsylvania town. It was the closest she ever got to going to college because of her marriage at a young age and caring for her young children never allowed her to pursue or develop that gift. She was a reader, though, sneaking a chapter here and there when the kids were asleep. Kids grown, she walked often to the neighborhood library to stock up on books, her favorite past time.

How cruel it seemed that it was her mind that went first. How lucky were we that her heart embraced us up to the end.

There have been many moments these last few years when I could not catch my breath and thought that I would suffocate from the thought of losing this lovely presence in my life. And then I remember her touch on my cheek and the words that I will never forget. And I breathe again.

My mother died today. But she is still here in the morning sun, in the first cup of freshly brewed coffee, in the wonder of a well written paragraph or chapter from a new book. She is here in her children and grandchildren. She is here in all she taught us. She is here in our memories and in our hearts. She is still here in all the things that mattered to her. And even though I would prefer the warmth of her physical presence, this will do for now.

And so I say, with love and gratitude, as I write about her today: This one, Mum, this one is for you.

Home to Each Other

I pulled into the familiar old driveway for what may have been the last time. I got to the house an hour early so that I would have time for a final pilgrimage. I went to every room, top to bottom, and thought about something familiar, something treasured in each room in order to see one last time what my heart would always remember. Then I sat on the front porch.

My mother had died six months before and my father had moved to an assisted living complex. As my dad's power of attorney, I was getting ready to sign a contract with a realtor to sell the home that had been in our family for more than forty years.

The front porch had been a special place for all of us in the family. It became the main room in the summer and fall. We all hung out there when we visited. Thankfully I had listened to my brother's suggestion to take the round, wooden picnic table that he had built. It had been on the large front porch for years. He loaded it onto his truck and delivered it to me a few weeks before the closing of the house.

I signed the papers and handed over all of the keys. Having done my duty, I backed out of the driveway and cried all the way home. For seventy miles I cried. And I remembered. And I gave thanks for all of the love, warmth and generosity that had happened in that house, in that home.

After exiting the freeway, I stopped at Home Depot for an important purchase. I knew it would be in hardware but I did not have the energy to look. An HD employee was on the top step of one of the big orange ladders.

"Can you point me to upholstery tacks," I asked, knowing that she could not detect my swollen eyes from that distance.

"Well, they are in the next aisle," she said, "but may take time to find. Let me get down from here and I will show you where they are located."

When she reached ground level she looked at me and asked, "Are you ok?"

"I will be when I get the tacks," I replied.

She took me directly to the little peg where they were hanging. After thanking her I went to the self-check out because I did not want anyone else to notice my distress.

I drove to my apartment building on Lake Erie and went directly to my balcony. I used the embroidery tacks to secure a flannel-backed tablecloth to the picnic table. Then I smiled and said to myself, "The house is gone. The table is not." And neither are the memories. And the home will never be gone. Is it not where the heart is?

Though it might be time to move on, I have plenty to take with me on the journey ahead. Not the least of which is an old picnic table with a brand new flannel backed tablecloth now sitting pretty on my windy balcony.

When my family visits in the summer and fall we hang out on the balcony. Around the table. We have become home to each other now. And we celebrate the comfort that we find in having an old picnic table to center us. An old picnic table with a new flannel backed tablecloth. Tacked down. Secure in whatever wind may blow.

Thank You

Happiness Is a Choice: A Special Thank You

"You were my first existential teacher," she said.

I had unexpectedly met her for breakfast twenty-five years after she had been a student in my class.

"What did I teach you that makes you say that?" I asked.

"You taught me that happiness is a choice and I have passed that on to all of my children," she answered.

I told her that I had that little piece of wisdom framed on my dresser to remind me every day of that lesson that I still try to own for myself. I still work at it twenty-five years later. And what a boost it was to me to know that something I had said so long ago was still alive in the family of this student of yesterday. This student who shared a cup of coffee and an encouraging conversation with a teacher who had taught her that happiness was a choice when she was a junior in high school.

This is not really about me or about that former student. This is for all of the teachers who teach with energy and with kindness. For all of the teachers who bid farewell to graduates and who do not have evidence that a few words they shared would live on in the families of their students.

Most of all this is for Mrs. von Shulick who taught me about writing when I was a sophomore at Ursuline High School in Youngstown, Ohio. She was a source of support for me more years ago than I am willing to report. She liked how and what I wrote and pushed me to write more. And then even more. I was taught that it was a craft that needed practice and she encouraged me to keep at it. All those many years ago. And I never told her what she meant to me.

I am telling you now Mrs. von Shulick wherever you are in the heavens. You made a difference and how I wish I had been able to tell you over a cup of coffee.

Somehow, though, I think you already know.

Personal Thanks To

Linda Amadeo, Executive Editor of Human Development Magazine, retired. Thank you for remembering and for being such a valuable mentor.

Maureen Tighe-Brown for being so generous with your time and with your critical eye. This book belongs to you, too.

Paulette Kirchensteiner, HM for your cover art and for being such a valued collaborator.

The following readers who read the manuscript as it was being written and who gave me valuable feedback:

My HM Sister readers who inspire me, who make me think and who make me laugh: Rose Bator, Catherine Cassidy, Rita Costello, Julie Demchak, Mary Hurley, Kathleen King, Rose Marie Kramer, Cheryl Rose, Cathy Walsh and Dorothy Zwick.

Stacy Dever for spotting a few critical gaps that needed to be filled.

Sam Fulwood III, Senior Fellow, The Center for American Progress, for allowing me to use his quote.

And finally, Mike Manning at Villa Beach Communications who made the last mile so easy.

Credits and Acknowledgements

The following chapters first appeared in Human Development Magazine:

"Lost in a World of Plenty," Volume 24, #3, Fall, 2003

"The Eighth Sacrament," Volume 24, #4, Winter, 2003

"Emily," Volume 25, #2, Summer, 2004

"Throwaway Kids," Volume 25, #3, Fall, 2004

"Beauty, Deep Beauty," Volume 26, #2, Summer, 2005

"Faithful Servant," Volume 26, #3, Fall, 2005

"The Other Side of Middle Age," Volume 26, #4, Winter, 2005

"The Hearts of Children," Volume 27, #2, Summer, 2006

"Home," Volume 28, #2, Summer, 2007

 "Common Grace," Volume 28, #4, Winter, 2007

"A Kirundi Hymn," Volume 29, #4, Fall, 2008

"A Giraffe Inside My Van," Volume 30, #1, Spring, 2009

The following first appeared in the National Catholic Reporter:

"Mother Cabrini's head prompts satori moment," March 5, 2004

Chapter 5: Emily
D. Haas, "Blest Are They," 1985
D. Schutte, "You Are Near," 1971
D. Schutte, "City of God," 1981

Chapter 15: There's a Giraffe in My Van
George D. Weiss and Bob Thiele, "What a Wonderful World," 1967.

Chapter 16: Mama Cass
John Phillips, "Go Where You Wanna Go," 1965.
John Phillips, "Monday, Monday," 1966.
William Robinson-Ronald White, "My Girl," 1964.
Barry Mann and Cynthia Weil, "Make Your Own Kind of Music," 1968.

Made in the USA
Lexington, KY
29 December 2010